# Peterhof
# Tsarskoye Selo
# Pavlovsk
# Oranienbaum
# Gatchina

D1511655

P-2 Art Publishers
St Petersburg

$\mathcal{T}$he majestic and beautiful image of St Petersburg, the city which has been preserved by Providence during the cataclysms of the twentieth century, is inseparable from the luxurious Imperial palace-and-park residences surrounding the northern capital of Russia — Peterhof, Tsarskoye Selo, Oranienbaum and Gatchina.

All these architectural complexes taken together build up an integral historical and artistic chronicle of Russian life and culture. But each of them also bears an imprint of the activities and personal tastes, predilections and antipathies of those monarchs who gave preference to this particular place as his or her favourite country residence.

The Peterhof palaces, fountains, cascades and regular parks dating from the eighteenth century are especially evocative of the turbulent, highly creative age of Peter the Great.

The palaces and parks of Tsarskoye Selo take us back to resplendent court ceremonies held during the successful reigns of Empress Elizabeth, Peter's daughter, and of Catherine the Great who ascended the throne soon after her. It is with the rule of Catherine the Great that the heyday of the residence at Oranienbaum, which incorporated the Great Palace of Prince Menshikov, Peter's outstanding companion-in-arms, is associated. Pavlovsk and Gatchina shed light on the personality of Paul, then the Heir Apparent and later the Emperor, and on the drama of his life. The architectural features of Alexandria and the Cottage Palace in Peterhof, as well as the park structures of Tsarskoye Selo, are illustrative of the reign of Nicholas I, his character and his political preferences. Gatchina was the favourite residence of Emperor Alexander III. His successor Nicholas II felt an equal attachment to Peterhof and Tsarskoye Selo and shared his time between them. His whole family permanently lived in the Alexander Palace at Tsarskoye Selo, whence the last Emperor of the ruling Romanov dynasty was forcibly deported after his abdication, together with his family, to Yekaterinburg where they met their tragic death. Therefore the royal residences in the environs of St Petersburg encompass the entire Imperial period in the history of Russia, from the inauguration of the Empire in 1721 to the end of the monarchy in 1917.

The Imperial summer residences in the environs of St Petersburg are unique assemblages of masterpieces of Baroque and Neo-Classical architecture illustrating these trends in all their variety and stylistic evolution. The regular and landscaped parks of these ensembles rival the best achievements in the art of landscape gardening.

The list of architects, sculptors and park designers engaged in their creation covers the whole history of Russian art in the eighteenth and nineteenth centuries. It is sufficient to remind that the palaces and parks were designed and decorated by such outstanding architects as Le Blond, Barolomeo Francesco Rastrelli, Charles Cameron, Vincenzo Brenna, Antonio Rinaldi, Yury Velten, Giacomo Quarenghi, Andrei Voronikhin, Jean-François Thomas de Thomon, Carlo Rossi, Vasily Stasov, Adam Menelaws and Andrei Stakenschneider.

In the changed social conditions of the twentieth century, the Imperial residences acquired the status of museums of history and art. But during the Second World War these treasure-houses of culture suffered great damage and seemed to have been lost for ever. However, Russia's indestructible creative potential has made it possible to recover the seemingly irreparable losses — thanks to the great talents and strenuous efforts of restorers the palaces have risen from the ashes and the saved authentic paintings have been gradually returned to the same display rooms.

Today, the immortal beauty of the palace-and-park ensembles which once served as Imperial residences continue to give aesthetic pleasure to people helping them overcome the tribulations of life and instilling a reverence for higher spiritual values.

# Peterhof

Peterhof, a coastal residence of the Russian Emperors which is famous the world over, has primarily become a symbol of the age of Peter the Great. The complex of palaces, fountains and decorative sculpture of the Lower Park and the Upper Gardens has epitomized the energy and creative enthusiasm of the period when Russia, led by the indomitable will of Peter the Great, received a powerful impetus for its future development.

A starting point in the chronology of Peterhof is exactly recorded in the *Travel Journal of Peter the Great*. The entry for 13 September 1705 reads that a small ship called *Munker* moored near an old farmstead which was chosen by Peter the Great as a recreation spot during sea outings and to which he gave his name. May 1714 saw the start of intense work on the construction of a state residence there. On 15 August 1723 Peter the Great marked the completion of the ambitious project by a sumptuous celebration during which the Great Cascade and sixteen fountains were inaugurated. The beauty of the newly built seaside residence amazed foreign guests, diplomats and entire St Petersburg. During the subsequent centuries the complex of Peterhof parks, palaces and fountains has been extended and enriched to become a place of fairy-tale beauty.

*T*he palace-and-park complex of Peterhof is one of those culminating artistic accomplishments of all the times and peoples which are describable as "wonders of the world". Every year for more than two centuries the palaces, fountains and parks of Peterhof delight its visitors from the early summer to the late autumn as an unforgettable spectacle in which the fascinating examples of architecture, landscape gardening and sculpture blend into a single triumphal accord. Every detail, every part of the Peterhof ensemble, an outstanding creation by noted European and Russian masters, adds to the its powerful artistic impact.

*Monument to Peter the Great. 1883–84. Sculptor Mark Antokolsky. Architect Eduard Hahn*

*The central ensemble of the Lower Park. The Great Cascade and the Pool (view from a helicopter)*

The Great Cascade is the heart of the Peterhof ensemble which conveys the idea of the celebration of Russia's victorious struggle for an exit to the sea. The Great Cascade, with its breathtaking blend of water effects and sculptural decor, was created according to the concept of Peter the Great to glorify the courage of Russian soldiers and sailors. Organically linked with the complex of the Great Cascade are the imposing palace erected above it, the Sea Canal and dozens of powerful fountains glistening with the gold of their statues, bas-reliefs and vases. The building and decoration of the Great Cascade — the dominant fountain structure of Peterhof — began in 1715 and lasted for seven years. The Tsar's ideas were creatively developed by the whole galaxy of celebrated architects including Alexander Le Blond, Johann Braunstein, Niccolo Michetti and Mikhail Zemtsov, as well as by the sculptor Carlo Bartolomeo Rastrelli and the fountain master Paul Sualem. The Great Cascade is unique for the plastic expressiveness of its architectural and sculptural forms and for a perfectly unified impression they produce which is largely due to whimsical, ever changing patterns of water jets and streams. Water is either falling down the abrupt cascade steps or gushing upwards violently, interweaving in arc-shaped curves or palpitating in iridescent designs, while its gentle murmur is filling the air.

←
*Panorama of the Great Palace, the Great Cascade and the Alley of Fountains*

*Perspective view of the Sea Canal*

*Decorative statue: **Mercury** 1800. Copy of an ancient original from the 2nd century B.C.*

Water increases a dynamic sweep of statuary and even enhances its conceptual significance. The Great Cascade includes two seven-step cascades flanking the central three-step waterfall stairway and seventy-five water-jets. One of the most impressive among them is the Basket Fountain located in the centre of the water pageant, in front of the Large Grotto. Twenty-eight oblique jets spurting from a tufa ring are interlacing like a tracery of a flower basket. Nine stems of fantastic flowers are fluttering within its crystal frame. They are resplendent like a festive bouquet brought, as it were, to the balcony of the Great Peterhof Palace.

The flanking cascades are elaborate architectural structures, the designs and scale of which determine the diverse play of light through the water amidst the gilded statues, vases, consoles and bas-reliefs. The streams of water are falling step by step from the height of twenty metres. The curving edges of the cascade risers lend to the streams a Baroque vivacity and profusion.

*Decorative sculpture:* **Perseus**. *1801*
*Sculptor Feodosy Shchedrin*

*Decorative statue:* **Galatea**. *1801*
*Sculptor Jean-Dominique Rachette*

*Decorative statue:* **Amazon**. *Copy from an*
*ancient original of the 5th–4th centuries B.C.*

In sharp contrast to them are the fourteen straight water jets shooting upwards at either side of each step. Their steep edges are richly decorated with bas-reliefs and corbels. On the parapets of the Cascade, mounted on marble pedestals are gilded bronze statues of ancient gods and heroes alternated with elaborate bronze bowls and vases . During the Petrine era the subject matter of the bas-reliefs and statues was interpreted as an allegory of glorious victories of Russia in the Northern War fought for the dominance over the Baltic shores, as well as a satire on the self-sufficient enemy — Sweden.

The decor of the Great Cascade includes 241 statues and other sculptural forms, each of which has an artistic value of its own while being an integral part of the entire composition. Linked with the Great Cascade is the Pool decorated at the sides by bronze sculptural fountain groups, *Sirens* and *Naiads*. In the middle of the Pool, on a granite rock pediment, soars the huge bronze sculptural group, *Samson Tearing Open the Jaws of the Lion* — a pathetic allegory of the victory of Russia's "Samson", Peter the Great, in the Battle of Poltava over

Charles XII of Sweden personified here
by the image implying the Swedish heraldic
lion. The *Samson* sculpture decorates the
tallest (21 metres) and most powerful
fountain of Peterhof. The first lead sculptural
group was produced in 1735 by Bartolomeo
Carlo Rastrelli to mark the 25th anniversary
of the Poltava victory. In 1801 it was replaced by a new *Samson* cast in bronze
after a model by Mikhail Kozlovsky.
Carried away by the invaders in 1942–43,
the statue was recreated by Vasily Simonov.
The Samson Fountain is a veritable masterpiece remarkable for a harmonious combination of decorative sculpture and the dynamic
water element.

*Sculptural decor of the Great Cascade*

*The Great Cascade. Decorative statue:*
**Ganymede**. *Copy of an ancient original*
*by Leochares. 1800*

The statuary decorating the Great Cascade has underwent major alterations. In the early nineteenth century lead effigies created during Peter's times were replaced by bronze casts. Seventeen of the new pieces of sculpture were modelled on ancient examples close to the originally installed statues in their plastic qualities and subject matter. Fifteen pieces were cast anew from models by the best Russian sculptors, professors of the Academy of Arts. Outstanding for their plastic perfection and emotional expressiveness are the statues of *Perseus* and *Sirens* created by Feodosy Shchedrin; *Alcides* by Ivan Prokofyev notable for its striking combination of dynamic and static

qualities; *Galatea* by Jean-Dominique Rachette remarkable for its subtlest lyricism, and *Pandora* executed after a model by Fedot Shubin. All of them add to the magnificence of the Great Cascade making it a unique artistic monument of world stature.

The Great Cascade is perceived as a great musical and choreographic performance in which everything is pervaded with a pathetic exultation and joy. The singing of water jets and the splashes of streams merge into a single hymn to the glory of Russia.

*The Great Cascade*
*The East Waterfall Stairway*

*The Great Cascade. The Samson Fountain*

The Monplaisir complex, Peter the Great's favourite recreation place, is located in the east section of the Lower Park. Originally this name (French for "my pleasure") was applied to the "small pavilions" erected by orders of Peter the Great on the shore of the Gulf of Finland. Over the years an unusual complex of gardens, fountains and decorative sculptures emerged around them. The main fountain structure of the Monplaisir area is the Dragon Cascade (also known as the Chessboard Hill Cascade). Its slopes are faced with tufa and the stairways are decorated at the sides with marble statues of ancient deities produced by Giovanni Bonazza and Filippo

Catasio. The parterre near the Chessboard Hill is adorned with the Roman Fountains designed in the early 1730s by the architects Ivan Davydov and Ivan Blank. They imitated the fountains standing in front of St Peter's in Rome, hence their names which were retained after they had been redesigned in granite and marble in 1798–1800 in the spirit of Classical architecture. Various kinds of coloured marble were used for their decoration, which was further enhanced by gilded masks, garlands and wreaths.

*The Roman Fountains*

*The Dragon (Chessboard Hill) Cascade*

*Sculpture:* **Dragons**

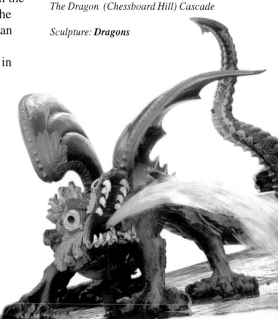

The ensemble of the east section of the Lower Park is distinguished by its unusual fountains each of which is truly unique. Most of them are trick fountains intended for amusing visitors. One of them is the Sun Fountain designed by Yury Velten in the 1770s. Another popular trick fountain, the famous Chinese Umbrella, amuses both children and grown-up people already for two centuries.

The Pyramid Fountain built in the first quarter of the eighteenth century has reached us without any major alterations. It is a truly unique example of the fountain designer's art from the age of Peter the Great. The palpitating, white foamy "pyramid" which resembles a liquid monument consists of 505 water jets soaring in seven tiers. Water, falling down the marble steps fills up the pool and in smooth, mirror-like streams pours to the basin around the fountain. The composition of the Pyramid Fountain is reigned by the pattern of water jets which is emphasized by the marble of the balustrade with vases and miniature bridges spanning the surrounding basin. The fountain designed by Niccolo Michetti is a development of the concept suggested by Peter the Great himself. The work was carried out in 1721–24.

The Pyramid Fountain never fails to amaze present-day visitors to Peterhof as it astonished Friedrich Wilhelm Bergholtz, the Kammer-Junker of the Duke of Holstein, who wrote about his visit to the Lower Park in the reign of Peter the Great: "There is hardly such a large and beautiful fountain anywhere else."

*The Pyramid Fountain*

*The Sun Fountain*

*T*he gem of Peterhof is Peter's favourite Monplaisir and its garden with fountains including two trick fountains dating back to the Petrine era. The brick masonry of the palace façade, its clear-cut and concise forms and its tent-shaped roof remind us about the Dutch tastes of Peter the Great.

*The Palace of Monplaisir*
*The Monplaisir Garden*
*The Sheaf Fountain*

*The Cloche Fountain*
*Sculpture:* **Psyche**. *1817*
*A copy from Antonio*
*Canova's original*

$\mathcal{T}$he Palace of Monplaisir was built in 1714–23 for Peter the Great after his sketches. Architecturally and artistically the palace was designed and decorated by the professional architects Braunstein, Le Blond and Michetti, the painter decorator Philippe Pillement, master craftsmen from the Moscow Armoury and icon-painters.

The State Hall, the main and largest interior of Monplaisir, as well as the galleries and rooms of the palace house Russia's first collection of Western European paintings assembled by Peter the Great. The Palace of Monplaisir is not only a very rare architectural monument, but also a witness to the age of great transformations, and this fact enables its visitors to sense a specific atmosphere of the first quarter of the eighteenth century.

*The Palace of Monplaisir. The East Gallery*

*The State Hall. Decorative sculpture:* **Spring.** *1720s. Sculptor Bartolomeo Carlo Rastrelli*

*The State Hall*

*A* remarkable feature of the east section of the Lower Park is that it is made up of small gardens, miniature ensembles with water jets as their central elements. One such ensemble is the Orangery Garden near the oval building of the Orangery. The stately edifice was erected in 1722–25 after Michetti's drawings by the architects Braunstein and Zemtsov who succeeded in endowing the utilitarian building with palatial features. In the centre of the Orangery Garden stands the fountain decorated with the sculpture *Triton Tearing Open the Jaws of a Sea Monster*. The subject is an allegory of Russia's sea victories in the Northern War. The battle scene is watched by four turtles symbolizing both the cardinal points and the states which passively participated in the coalition war against Sweden. The initially installed lead group was produced by Bartolomeo Carlo Rastrelli. 150 years later it was replaced with a new one produced after a drawing by David Jensen in Berlin. The original concept, however, was then distorted — the mythical monster was replaced by a composition with a naturalistic crocodile. This composition was plundered during the Second World War and in postwar years the original sculptural group has been recreated after eighteenth-century drawings by the sculptor Alexei Gurdzhy.

*The Ramp, an entry to the Lower Park*

*The Orangery Fountain*
*The sculptural group: **Triton Tearing Open the Jaws of a Sea Monster***

The Hermitage, a small palace or pavilion, is located in the west section of the Lower Park, on the very coast of the Gulf of Finland. It was built to the design of Johann Braunstein in 1721–25. The pavilion was intended for a secluded rest of the Emperor and persons close to him. It owes its name to the French word *hermitage* meaning the habitation of a recluse. The palace's isolated position was provided by a man-made ditch around it with a drawbridge which connected the structure with the surrounding world.

The entire upper floor of the pavilion was occupied from 1759 by the Hall decorated with paintings by Flemish, Dutch, French, Italian and German artists of the seventeenth and eighteenth centuries. The history painting *The Battle of Poltava* (1727) was produced by the Russian artist Ivan Nikitin. In the middle of the Hall stands an oval table for fourteen diners. Servants and cooks who prepared meals on the ground floor used a special mechanism to lift the central section of the dining-table laid with all kinds of dishes. Any guest could order a special dish to his or her choice by ringing a hand-bell.

The Hermitage Pavilion is a very rare monument of architecture and art dating from the first quarter of the eighteenth century and recreating the atmosphere of intimate conversations characteristic of the "gallant" age. It belongs to the category of amusement pavilions popular in regular European gardens of the seventeenth and eighteenth centuries and intended for a brief pleasing relaxation in the course of promenades. The architecture of the Hermitage Pavilion is marked by a harmony of proportions. The tall windows with numerous small panes illuminate the Hall and afford a view of the sea and the park around the building both from the interior and through the pavilion.

*The Hermitage Pavilion*

*The Hermitage Pavilion. The Hall*

The spatial composition of the Lower Park is consistently based on the principle of symmetry. This principle can be traced in the placement of companion fountains, similar in their artistic features, at the intersections of the avenues and in front of the cascades. At the corners of the Great Parterre flower beds, by the foot of the Great Cascade, are the Marble Bench Fountains with the statues of *Nymph* and *Danaid* created according to a concept by Andrei Stakenschneider in 1854. The Adam and Eve Fountains designed by Peter the Great himself can rival their most famous Peterhof counterparts. They are decorated with marble statues specially commissioned for Russia from the Venetian sculptor Giovanni Bonazza. The Adam Fountain began to operate in 1722 and the Eve Fountain was completed in 1726. Equidistant from the Great Cascade and the Sea Canal, the Adam and Eve Fountains mark the compositional pivots of the west and east sections of the Lower Park. The artistic effect of the fountains is created by sixteen curving jets of water. They echo the octagonal pool with eight radiant avenues diverging from it and affording numerous perspective views.

*The Marble Bench Fountain:* **Danaid**

*The Eve Fountain*

*View of the Marly Palace*

*The Golden Hill Cascade*

The Marly ensemble is situated in the west section of the Lower Park. The name was borrowed by Peter the Great from the French royal residence which admired him during his visit by its system of water supply to a cascade, ponds and pavilions. However, the Marly ensemble in Peterhof, as it follows from Peter the Great's own sketches and his decrees, was not a literal copy of its French model, the Marly-le-Roi residence. It has rather become a free improvisation on the subject of its French prototype. The dominant structure of the complex — the Marly Cascade or the Golden Hill — was built in 1722–23 by Michetti, Braunstein, Zemtsov and Usov. In 1731–32 Zemtsov imparted a more up-to-date air to the Cascade — the waterfall steps (there are twenty-one of them) were covered with gilded copper plates and decorated with sculptures on the parapets and attics.

The Marly Cascade is decorated with three Medusa mascarons produced by Bartolomeo Carlo Rastrelli in 1724 and with marble statues carved in the early eighteenth century by Pietro Baratta, Giovanni Zorzoni and A. Garcia.

The Marly complex, a model
of regular planning in the French
fashion, was created in 1720–24.
The design of the two-storey Marly
Palace, a work by Johann Braunstein, was amended in the course of
the construction by Peter the Great
himself. In front of the west façade
of the palace are located four sec-
torial ponds, in front of the east one,
the large Marly Pond. Avenues
diverge from it like the points of
a trident crossing the entire Lower
Park from the west to the east.
To the north and south of the pond
are laid out gardens protected from
the seashore by an earthen rampart.
One of these gardens is dedicated
to Bacchus and adorned with the
Triton Cloche and Menazherny
(Economical) Fountains.

*The Golden Hill Cascade.*
*Decorative sculpture:* **Neptune**. *1860s*

*Panorama of the Marly ensemble*

*The Great Palace. The Armorial Block*

$\mathcal{T}$he large-scale Great Palace, glistening with the gilded cupolas of its wings, stands out among all other structures in the Peterhof ensemble. With its front facing the sea, it makes up, together with the Great Cascade, a single majestic monument to the eighteenth-century Russian Empire. Originally, in 1714–24, Braunstein, Le Blond and Michetti built the modest Upper Mansion. In 1745–55, Rastrelli, put in charge of its reconstruction by Empress Elizabeth Petrovna, rebuilt it into a majestic palace combining the features of the Petrine and Elizabethan Baroque. The architect extended the building adding galleries on either side and effectively completing them with two-storey wings. The final element of the west wing was the Church consecrated to the Apostles Peter and Paul and the east wing ended with the Armorial Block.

The state interiors of the Great Palace were decorated by Rastrelli with an especial luxury. The gilded wooden sculpture, high-relief decoration, ornaments, inlaid parquetry, polychrome ceiling paintings, pictorial insets, tempera decorations and damask fabrics reflected in the numerous mirrors and brightly illuminated from the wide windows, all contributed to an impression of unusual resplendence.

The great Rastrelli was at his best in the designs of the State Staircase, the Audience Room and the Ballroom (or Merchant Room). Ornamental fantasies of the architect were perfectly realized by French and Russian carvers who combined their national artistic traditions in this work.

The suite of halls and reception rooms created after drawings by Rastrelli, seems to entice the visitor to the palace into a brilliant, fascinating realm. The architect used characteristic Baroque elements in the decor of all the interiors. Nevertheless each detail was given a distinctive treatment and the decorative design of every single room and hall bears some special features of its own. The suite design of the palace corresponded to the ceremonial mode of life of the Russian Imperial court which resembled a sumptuous theatrical pageant. The splendour of the Great Palace, which witnessed the two-century history of the state, was a result of creative work by outstanding architects such as Braunstein, Le Blond, Michetti, Rastrelli, Velten and Stakenschneider.

*The State Staircase of the Great Palace*
*Allegorical sculpture:* **Summer**. *1751*
*Architect Bartolomeo Francesco Rastrelli*

*The State Staircase of the Great Palace*

*The Great Palace. The Audience Hall*

*The Great Palace. The Throne Room*

*The Throne Room. The Imperial throne
Early 18th century*

*Vigilius Erichsen. **The March of
Catherine the Great to Peterhof.** 1762*

*J*n 1763–80 the Throne Room and a number of other interiors of the Great Palace acquired a new look which suited the Classicist tastes of Empress Catherine the Great. In the Throne Room, the moulded decor was redesigned after drawings by Yury Velten and the longitudinal walls between the top-light windows were embellished with twelve painted portraits of Peter the Great's relatives. Over the four doors leading to the room were placed formal likenesses of Peter the Great, Catherine I, Anna Ioannovna and Elizabeth Petrovna, while the equestrian portrait of Catherine the Great showing her during the memorable march from St Petersburg to Peterhof in 1762 began to grace the east wall, above the throne.

The Portrait (or Picture) Room is located in the very centre of the Great Palace. During the Petrine age it was known as the Italian Salon and was thought to be the most imposing interior in the palace. In the middle of the eighteenth century the doors of the room were adorned with magnificent carved ornament after sketches by Rastrelli. In 1764 Jean-Baptiste Vallin de la Mothe redesigned the decor of the room covering its walls with paintings by Pietro Rotari. All the 368 original works have survived and after restoration of the room they have been returned to their former places.

*The Great Palace. The Portrait Room*

*The Great (Blue) Drawing Room*

*The Banquet Service. 1848–52*
*The Imperial Porcelain Factory,*
*St Petersburg*

*The Great Palace*
*The West Chinese Lobby*

*The West Chinese Lobby*
*Tiled stove*

𝒯he Chinese Lobbies of the Great Peterhof Palace are located at either side of the Portrait Room. They owe their names to the type of their decoration which catered the tastes of the eighteenth century with its vogue for Chinese art. The decorator of the East and West Chinese Lobbies, Vallin de la Mothe, used in the trimming of their walls the painted panels of authentic lacquered Chinese screens. He added them with lacquer insets of a Russian work stylized in the *chinoiserie* spirit. Even the ceilings of the interiors painted in lacquers are given a porcelain-like texture. Of especial value are the parquet floors inlaid of amaranth, rosewood, sandal, ebony and other precious kinds of wood. The decor of the Chinese Lobbies was recreated after the Second World War.

*The Upper Gardens. The Neptune Fountain*

*Panoramic view of the Upper Gardens*

The Upper Gardens stretch in front of the south façade of the Great Palace. They were laid out in a regular manner according to sketches by Peter the Great and drawings by Le Blond, Braunstein and the master gardener Leonard van Harnigfelt in 1724. Towards 1739 the architects Mikhail Zemtsov, Ivan Blank and Ivan Davydov as well as the sculptor Bartolomeo Carlo Rastrelli attained a perfect symmetry in the layout of this formal garden introducing five fountains with lead sculptural groups there. In the latter half of the eighteenth century the sculptural decor was altered. However, the Square Pools, the Great Pond and two round pools created in the 1730s have survived to this day. The largest fountain of the Upper Gardens is *Neptune* depicting the sea god with a fantastic retinue. The bronze group including more than thirty figures is an outstanding work produced by Nuremberg sculptors in the 1650s and 1660s. In the late eighteenth century the complex was acquired by Emperor Paul I for Gatchina, but eventually it was installed in the Upper Gardens as a befitting decoration for one of the most beautiful Peterhof fountains.

The so-called Alexandria area, the seaside residence of Nicholas I, adjoins the east border of the Lower Park. The lands of the future Alexandria were presented by Emperor Alexander I to his brother Grand Duke Nikolai Pavlovich, who in December 1825 ascended the Russian throne. On becoming the single owner of all the royal residences, Nicholas I presented this plot of land to his wife, Empress Alexandra Fiodorovna. The building of the new Imperial residence, which received the name of "Alexandria, Her Majesty's Dacha", was carried out very intensively and with a great sweep. An extensive landscaped park was being laid out, for which thousands of various trees and rare bushes were brought, roads were being built and the construction of all sorts of buildings was under way. Nicholas I entrusted Adam Menelaws, the Scottish architect, with the fulfillment of this project. His designs were used in 1826–29 to erect a palace which was named the "Cottage" or "Country House" in the English manner. Its fronts, interiors and furnishings reflect the general European romantic interest in mediaeval art, preeminently the Gothic perceived in the spirit of Walter Scott.

The Cottage Museum Palace affords a glimpse of the private life of Emperor Nicholas I, the spiritual world of his family permeated with a warmth of feeling and full of romantic comfort.

*Alexandria. The Cottage Palace*

*The Cottage Palace. The Drawing Room of Empress Alexandra Fiodorovna*

*The Cathedral of the SS Apostles Peter and Paul in Peterhof. 1895–1904 Architect Nikolai Sultanov, with the participation of V. Kosiakov*

# Tsarskoye Selo

Tsarskoye Selo — the very name of this palace-and-park ensemble provokes a number of happy recollections. In addition to its beautiful parks and architecture, it is also associated with the great age of Russian poetry and the ceremonial glamour of the past autocratic life. In the seventeenth century, there was the Swedish farmstead Saritsa, later renamed *Saris hoff*, in this area. The Finnish name of the farmstead was *Saaris moisio* ("a farmstead on the elevation") and its Russianized form was *Sarskaya myza*. After Russia had eventually taken hold of these lands, Sarskaya myza (or Sarskoye Selo) became the property of Alexander Menshikov, and from 1708 to 1724 it was the summer residence of Peter the Great's wife, Yekaterina Alexeyevna. In 1711, after Catherine was declared "the true Sovereign", the building of a large-scale residence began on the site. Johann Braunstein and Johann Christian Förster were mainly responsible for its construction. Catherine I bequathed Sarskoye Selo to her daughter, Tsesarevna Elizabeth Petrovna. On becoming the Empress in 1741, she, with her innate breadth of nature, did not spare funds for turning the old mansion into a luxurious palace, for building various pavilions and for laying-out gardens. In 1743–51 the Empress's projects for the extension of the suburban residence were carried out by Mikhail Zemtsov, Andrei Kvasov and Savva Chevakinsky. In 1752–56, the work on the estate, by then already renamed Tsarskoye Selo, or the Tsars' Village, was supervised by Bartolomeo Francesco Rastrelli. It was he who gave to the palace and the entire complex that luxurious Baroque appearance which was poetically compared with a "celestial constellation". During the reign of Catherine the Great Tsarskoye Selo was further enriched with the works of the architects Antonio Rinaldi, Yury Velten, Vasily Neyelov, Charles Cameron and Giacomo Quarenghi, whose tastes were formed under the influence of ancient architecture.

It is the Catherine Palace, however, the fronts of which extend for 740 metres, that dominates the entire complex of Tsarskoye Selo. Its powerful decorative forms determine the plastic expressiveness of the palace endowing it with a truly regal majesty. This impression is enhanced by the interiors of the palace the decor of which reflects the swiftly changing tastes of the crowned owners. They are recorded in the decorative styles of the rooms and halls where Baroque luxury can be met side by side with Classical elegance.

The Great Hall (or the Ballroom) is a true masterpiece of the decorative genius of Rastrelli. This is one of the largest palatial halls created by this outstanding architect in St Petersburg and its environs in the 1750s. The hall's area is 846 square metres (it is seventeen metres wide and forty-seven metres long). The impression of its great expanse is still further enhanced thanks to the illusion of space created by the two tiers of windows. The piers between the windows are covered with mirrors in gilded carved frames. A sense of lightness is increased by the mirrors imitating windows on the butt-end walls and set in the piers and on the doors. The painted ceiling and the elaborate pattern of the inlaid parquet floor also add to the striking effect of the Ballroom. Nevertheless the predominant decorative element of the interior is gilded carving. Countless figures and half-figures, ornamental interlaces, cartouches and rocailles produce an indelible impression on visitors by their fantastic ingenuity and mastery of their execution.

←←

*The Great Palace. The garden front*

←

*The Great Palace. The garden front
Central part*

*The Great Hall (Ballroom)*

*The Great Hall. Overdoor decoration*

The Picture Hall, an interior the decor of which is largely devoted to painting, is characteristic of the first half of the eighteenth century. The powerful decorative effect created by tapestry-like hanging of the canvases combines here with the image of a picture gallery, an indispensable attribute in the home of an enlightened aristocrat during that period. Rastrelli completely covered the longitudinal walls with 130 paintings by Luca Giordano, Emmanuel de Witte, Adriaen van Ostade, David Teniers and other eminent Western European artists of the seventeenth and eighteenth centuries. Two paintings, *The Battle of Poltava* and *The Battle of Lesnaya*, were commissioned by Peter the Great from the French painter Pierre Denis Martin.

A veritable gem of the Catherine Palace was the Amber Study which is justly ranked by connoisseurs among "treasures of the world". In 1701–09 Gottfried Wolfram, Gottfried Tarau and Ernst Schacht produced, after a design by Andreas Schlüter, the inlaid amber panels which in 1717 were presented by Frederick William of Prussia to Peter the Great for the decoration of the Study in his third Winter Palace at St Petersburg. In 1755 Rastrelli designed the Amber Room in the Catherine Palace enriching the famous panels with Florentine mosaics and sculpture. Plundered by the Nazi soldiers during the Second World War, the amber decoration of the Study has nowadays been almost completely restored.

*The Amber Study*

*The Picture Room*

The Blue Drawing Room is the central apartment of the north section of the palace which was allotted by Catherine the Great to Grand Duke Pavel Petrovich, the heir to the throne, and his wife Maria Fiodorovna. Catherine the Great commissioned the designing of the heir's apartments, which included such interiors as the Green Dining Room, the Waiters' Room, the Blue Drawing Room, the Blue Chinese Drawing Room, the Bedroom and the Choir Anteroom, to the Scottish architect Charles Cameron, who brilliantly coped with the task. The Blue Drawing Room is one of the most remarkable interiors in the palace created by Cameron in the 1780s. Notable features of this interior are the silk upholstery of its walls adorned with a printed pattern, the artistic paintings of the ceilings and doors as well as the inlaid parquet floor. In all this majestic spectacle free improvisations of motifs borrowed from ancient art can be traced. Set into the moulded frieze with a gilded relief ornament are painted medallions featuring ancient images. The ceiling of the Blue Drawing Room is embellished with decorative painting based on semi-circles, rectangles and squares. Painted within the geometrical figures are mythological scenes and characters. The rich design of the inlaid parquet floor matches the elaborate compositional forms of the painted ceiling.

The decor of the Blue Drawing Room echoes the design of the Blue Chinese Drawing Room. Its walls are lined from top to bottom with blue silk which is embellished with stylized scenes of "Chinese life" painted in varicoloured inks. It is remarkable that Cameron, a convinced Classicist, combined the *chinoiserie* upholstery of the walls with ancient motifs of the ceiling painting, which lent the interior an air of artistic originality. The silk used for lining the walls in the reign of Catherine the Great was brought from China, but it was destroyed during the Second World War. The lost fabrics were recreated by restorers on the basis of a surviving sample.

*The Blue Drawing Room*

*The Chinese Blue Drawing Room*

*Detail of the upholstery
of the Chinese Blue Drawing Room*

$\mathcal{T}$he Bedroom of Maria Fiodorovna is one of the most spectacular
interiors created by Cameron in
the Catherine Palace. The architectural image of this room combined
the intimate character of a private
apartment with the luxury of a state
room. Cameron used for the decor
of the Bedroom moulded wall
panels executed by Ivan Martos,
which allegorically personified joy
and happiness of family life.
But the most prominent feature
of the Bedroom are thin faience
columns of the alcove. Lavishly
ornamented and emphasized by
golden strips and flutes, they seem
to have come down from the murals
of the Pompeiian villas.

*Detail of the Bedroom doors*

*The Bedroom*

The Green Dining Room, also decorated after drawings by Cameron, represents a version of the subtle interpretation of ancient motifs in the Russian interiors of the 1780s. Cameron had a profound knowledge of ancient art and in this work he freely improvised on the subject of ancient Roman decorative motifs. He attainedthe harmony of his artistic solution primarily by the use of plastic elements. The moulded details are arranged against the light green background of the walls with a thorough calculation. The main field is enlivened by a stylized representation of garden gates with medallions and moulded figures of youths and girls, seemingly supporting bas-reliefs with scenes of playing Cupids. The crowning element of the wall composition are arc-shaped twigs of vine.

The delicate tracery of details and the jeweller's modelling of sculptural forms executed by Ivan Martos after Cameron's drawings lend the Green Dining Room that sense of elegance which dominates the living apartments of the Catherine Palace.

*The Green Dining Room*

*The State Staircase. The Upper Landing*

→
*Perspective view of the garden front of the Great Palace*

The Grotto Pavilion (The Morning Hall)

The Hermitage Pavilion

The Upper Bath Pavilion

Sculpture: **Galatea**
Early 18th century
Sculptor Pietro Baratta

The regular garden laid out in front of the south façade of the Catherine Palace was created according to the concept of Bartolomeo Francesco Rastrelli. The architect included into his composition two garden pavilions: the Hermitage and the Grotto. Their complex plan, a play of volumes, plastic expressiveness of the silhouette and the saturated sculptural and ornamental decor emphasize the image of the pavilions which served as an "abode" for solitary repose and amusements of royal persons and their closest circle.

Rastrelli endowed the Hermitage Pavilion with such a decorative majesty that it began to resemble a miniature palace. Traditionally, the lower storey of the Hermitage Pavilion had mechanisms which were used to lift laid tables for meals held in the Central Hall of the upper floor. As a rule the procedure began in the very heat of a ball. The floors would suddenly open and exquisite dishes would appear from below to the guests' pleasant surprise.

The Grotto Pavilion built by Rastrelli on the bank of the Great Pond was used for recreation during boating parties. The pavilion's location and designation determined its fairy-tale moulded decor with sea monsters, dolphins and sea-shells. Unlike the emphatically decorative pavilions in the Baroque style, Classicist architects lent to garden structures geometrically clear-cut shapes accentuated by relief insets. Such is the Upper Bath Pavilion built in the 1770s by the architect Ilya Neyelov.

The Cameron Gallery created by Charles Cameron, an outstanding interpreter of ancient motifs, is called an architectural "poem" in the spirit of Classicism. The royal commissioner Catherine the Great formulated the idea of the project as a "Graeco-Roman rhapsody". And Cameron incarnated her dream with virtuoso mastery in 1783–87. The Cameron's Gallery, as Pushkin defined it, recalls a "huge hall" soaring towards clouds and dominating the Catherine Gardens. The stairway leading to it is striking for the rounded shape of its flights enhancing the impression that the white colonnade is hovering over the malachite of age-old tree crowns. There are fifty-four bronze busts of outstanding ancient Greeks installed in the Gallery, with the Russian scholar and poet Mikhail Lomonosov placed in the same row. In 1780–87 Cameron erected the building of the Cold Baths as a single ensemble with the Gallery. The volume and façades of the Cold Baths appear from the side of the gallery as a small pavilion, but from the side of the park it looks like a massive structure. The fronts of the Cold Baths are decorated with bronze and stone statues. The interiors of the upper floor are called the Agate Rooms. They are faced with plaques of coloured stone, mainly marble and jasper of various types and shades. The noble colours of natural stones determine the unique designs of the Amber and Agate Studies and of the Great Hall testifying to the exclusive taste of the architect, sculptors and stone carvers who created this unique ensemble.

*The Cameron Gallery*
*Perspective view of the colonnade*

*The Agate Pavilion. The Great Hall*

*The Cameron Gallery. The State Stairway*

The Ramp of the Cameron Gallery leads to the landscaped section of the Catherine Park. The architect treated it in the manner of ancient cyclopean structures like aqueducts, open waterways of Ancient Rome. The powerful, gradually descending arches divided by semicircular supports-columns bear the gently sloping descent which is linked to the Ramp Avenue. The keystones of the arches are emphasized by masks of mythological creatures carved of stone. These mascarons are unique examples of Russian decorative sculpture of the late eighteenth century. The composition of the Ramp was completed with bronze statues in 1794. Later, by order of Paul I, they were moved to Pavlovsk, and in 1828 decorative bowls reminiscent of ancient lamps were installed to replace them. The Ramp forms an effective perspective along the middle axis and produces an impression of a complex of triumphal arches from the side.

*Keystone mask*

*Cameron's Ramp*

The landscaped section of the Catherine Park is situated around the Great Pond. A number of unique park pavilions are connected with it, among which the Turkish Bath reminiscent of a miniature mosque is prominent. It was built to a design by Hypolitto Monighetti in 1850–52. The most famous monument to Catherine the Great, the Chesme Rostral Column, soars on a small island of the Great Pond. It was erected to a design by Antonio Rinaldi in 1774–76 to commemorate the victory of the Russian squadron over the Turkish fleet in Chesme Bay in the Aegean Sea in 1770. A whole complex of buildings in the Chinese fashion was put up on the orders of Catherine the Great at the border of the Catherine and Alexander Parks — the Chinese Village, the Great and Small Caprices and several bridges. One of them was built at the south corner of the Cross Canal. The Creaking Pavilion was erected nearby to the design of Yury Velten. This pavilion crowned with weather-vanes attracted visitors' attention primarily by its unusual *chinoiserie* decoration. A complex of "Chinese amusements" was increased by the construction of a group of the so-called Chinese Bridges created in the late 1770s and early 1780s. Besides the Cross Bridge, there are four of them — the Dragon Bridge, two iron Chinese bridges and the Large Stone Bridge.

*The Cross Bridge*

*The Great Caprice*

*The Creaking Pavilion*

*The Great Pond. The Turkish Bath*

*The Chesme Column*

*A* notable structure in the Catherine Park which invariably attracts visitors' attention is the bridge known under three different names — the Palladian, Marble or Siberian Bridge. The first name is connected with the Roman architect Andrea Palladio who created a prototype of the Tsarskoye Selo bridge, while the second and third ones refer to the material, Siberian marble, which Vasily Neyelov used to built this park structure.

The fountain *The Milkmaid, or Girl with a Pitcher* has been celebrated by poets. Its spring is covered by a granite boulder crowned with the bronze figure of a young girl crying over the broken pitcher.

*The Palladian Bridge*

*The Ruin Tower. 1773. Architect Yury Velten*

*Fountain:* **The Milkmaid, or Girl with a Pitcher**. *1817. Sculptor Pavel Sokolov*

*T*he Golden Gate decorates the main entrance to the Catherine Palace. Behind it, in keeping with the tradition of eighteenth-century architecture, is the formal courtyard arranged in front of the main north façade of the palace. In 1745–51 Chevakinsky and Kvasov adorned the Formal Courtyard with semicircular service wings called "circumferences". In 1752–56 Rastrelli clad the Circumferences into sumptuous Baroque "garments" having stylistically united the service blocks with the courtyard. Put up in the gaps between them were fences and gates with pylons. The pattern of the railings and gates brilliantly revealed the architect's ingenuity and talent. The graphic silhouette of the forged frame is enhanced and completed by a variety of elaborate gilded scrolls, garlands, sea-shells, feathers and stars. The design of the gates and the sections of the railings show the emphasis on symmetry, but the openwork elegance of each detail adds to the pierced design a sense of ease and perfection. The Main Gates are crowned with the Imperial coat-of-arms, the gilded double-headed eagle, which emphasizes the designation of Tsarskoye Selo as a royal residence.

*The Catherine Palace*
*The Central "Golden" Gate*

*The railing of the palace. The Great Gate*

The Alexander Palace built by Catherine the Great as a gift to her first and favourite grandson Alexander Pavlovich (the future Alexander I) on the occasion of his wedding to Grand Duchess Elizabeth Alexeyevna, née the Baden Princess Luise-Marie-Augusta. Carrying out the Imperial commission, Giacomo Quarenghi created in 1792–96 one of the most perfect landmarks of world architecture the significance of which is not subject to the influence of time. The palace largely owes its rare magnificence to the double colonnade uniting the extending parts of the north front, with a happily found rhythm of the "movement" of slender shafts crowned by the capitals of the Corinthian order. Although Alexander I almost did not live in the palace on his accession to the throne,

this great creation by Cameron bears his name. During the reign of Nicholas I, however, it became the favourite residence of the Emperor's family who lived in Alexandria from the early spring till the end of May and after a short stay at Krasnoye Selo during manoeuvres returned to the Alexander Palace to spend their time there until the late autumn. Nicholas I had some rooms and the park redesigned in the then fashionable Romantic manner. Later Emperor Alexander III had his apartments in the right-hand wing of the palace.

The Alexander Palace began to play a particularly important role in the reign of Nicholas II. The Imperial family moved to the palace in 1905 and since then permanently lived there. The Alexander Palace became the official royal residence, a symbol of the last Emperor of Russia. It is with the Alexander Palace that the last days of the Romanov dynasty are connected — here in 1917 the final act of the drama connected with the crush of the Russian Empire was played. These crucial historic events gave to the masterpiece of architecture, the Alexander Palace, the status of a historical memorial.

In 1910–12 Vladimir Pokrovsky and Stepan Krichinsky erected for Nicholas II near the Alexander Palace the Cathedral of St Theodore which became the focal centre of the closed royal town. Its architecture reproduced the imagery and decorative motifs of ancient Russian Orthodox churches.

Tsarskoye Selo, which Pushkin associated in his verses with the idea of homeland, became the holy land of Russian poetry for subsequent generations. There are many buildings in Tsarskoye Selo connected with Pushkin's life — the house of Ludwig Wilhelm Tepper de Ferguson, a music teacher in the Lyceum, and the mansion of Vasily Malinovsky and Yegor Engelgardt, its first directors, the house of the writer and historian Nikolai Karamzin, and the famous Kitayeva's dacha which now houses a Pushkin museum. The poet lived at the dacha together with his young wife in 1831. But it is the Lyceum that evokes especially vivid associations connected with the poet's youth spent at Tsarskoye Selo. In 1811 the for-mer palatial wing, linked in 1789–91 with the Great Palace by a gallery, was given to the newly founded privileged educational establishment named the Lyceum. Here Alexander Pushkin studied between 1811 and 1817. At the graduation examination the young poet recited his poem *Recollections of Tsarskoye Selo* which brought the well-known writer and statesman Gavriil Derzhavin into raptures. Pushkin devoted to the Lyceum and Tsarskoye Selo, where "the Muse appeared" to him for the first time, a number of beautiful verses. To commemorate the Lyceum years of Pushkin in honour of the centenary of the poet's birth, on 2 May 1899 a monument to the poet was laid down in the Lyceum garden. It was cast of bronze after a model by the sculptor Robert Bach and opened a year later. The inhabitants of Tsarskoye Selo collected funds for the creation of the monument which has recorded for ever their love for the poetic genius of Russia.

*View of the Palace Church and the Lyceum*

*Monument to Alexander Pushkin
in the Lyceum Garden. 1900
Sculptor Robert Bach*

*Domes of the Church of the Palace*

# Pavlovsk

Pavlovsk, one of the most perfect works of architecture and the art of landscape gardening, occupies a special place among royal residences in the environs of St Petersburg. Its name reminds us of a complicated and largely tragic personality of Catherine the Great's son, Emperor Paul I. The early history of Pavlovsk, which was presented by the Empress to the heir to the throne Grand Duke Pavel Petrovich and his consort Maria Fiodorovna at the end of the 1770s, turned out to be closely related to their dramatically changing destinies. The date of the foundation of "the village of Pavlovskoye" is taken to be the year 1779 when two summer houses, the *Marienthal* ("Marie's Valley" after the name of Maria Fiodorovna) and the *Paullust* (Paul's pleasure") were

built. At the same time a small park with decorative structures, cascades and bridges was laid out. In 1780–85 Charles Cameron began the formation of the heir's royal residence. He built the Palace, the Temple of Friendship, the Apollo Colonnade and the Pavilion of the Three Graces. In 1796–1801, when Pavlovsk became the Imperial summer residence, the Palace was extended and its rooms were given a new, stately appearance. In the park the Old and New Sylvia areas were laid out, the Peel Tower and the Ruin Cascade were set up. After the death of Paul I Pavlovsk turned into a summer residence of the Dowager Empress Maria Fiodorovna. In 1802–25 such outstanding architects as Voronikhin, Quarenghi and Thomas de Thomon worked there.

$\mathcal{T}$he Palace is the predominant structure of the Pavlovsk ensemble. It was not accidental that the site for it was chosen on the high bank of the Slavianka and the natural elevation served as a podium for the building. The ceremony of its foundation took place on 25 May 1782 and its construction was basically finished towards the summer of 1786.

←

*The Pavlovsk Palace*
*View from the Bridge of Centaurs*

*The Pavlovsk Palace. Monument to Paul I*
*1851. Sculptor Ivan Vitali*

*View of the Pavlovsk Palace from a helicopter*

→

*The Pavlovsk Palace and the Parade Ground*

Charles Cameron, the designer of the project, gave to the building classically austere proportions reducing the decor of the façades to Corinthian columns and minor relief ornaments. The central part of the palace is crowned with a drum surrounded by a ring of sixty-four columns and supporting a low dome. In the 1780s and early 1790s the interiors of the ground floor — the Ballroom, the White Dining Room, the Old Drawing Room and the Billiards Room — were decorated to designs by Cameron. The upper floor where the Halls of War and Peace, the State Bedroom, the Italian Hall and the Grecian Hall were decorated before 1793 to designs by Vincenzo Brenna. In 1803–04 Andrei Voronikhin recreated and partly refashioned the interiors of the central part of the palace destroyed by a fire. In 1822–24 Carlo Rossi arranged a Library Hall named after him on the upper floor and redesigned some rooms of the ground floor. A major contribution to the decoration of palace interiors was made by the sculptors Mikhail Kozlovsky, Ivan Prokofyev, Vasily Demuth-Malinovsky, Ivan Martos and Fiodor Gordeyev, the artists Henri-François-Gabriel Viollier and Giovanni Scotti. The architectural and artistic overture to state rooms of the first floor are the Lower and Upper Vestibules. The Egyptian (Lower) Vestibule, designed by Cameron, is accentuated by allegorical statues of the twelve months. To match the statues, the walls are decorated with medallions showing the Zodiac signs. The Upper Vestibule on the first floor is decorated with antique military attributes and thematically matching frescoes.

*The Pavlovsk Palace. The Egyptian Vestibule*

*The State Staircase*

The Italian Hall, the compositional and artistic centre of the palace,
is a model of Classicist architectural design striking for its harmony
and elegance of proportions, exquisite symmetry and perfection of
the decor. The two-tiered volume of
the hall is crowned with a "hovering" dome. The austere centric
design of the palace is enlivened by
the semicircular and square niches
over which are running arched
apertures of the first-floor choirs
accentuated by a balustrade. The
piers between the choir arches are
decorated with caryatids bearing
the cornice of the dome and the
bas-relief representations of eagles
with outstretched wings. In the
decor of the hall are employed
authentic low-reliefs by Roman
sculptors of the first and second
centuries B.C.; set in niches are
ancient statues. The Italian Hall —
a work of art which has combined
the creative efforts of Cameron,
Brenna, Quarenghi and Voronikhin
— is remarkable for a subtle
colouring of the dome, the lilac
walls of artificial marble, the
ormolu mounts and rosewood
panelling of the doors. In the south
wing of the palace Brenna placed
the Picture Gallery, semicircular in
plan, with double-sided illumina-
tion. Such design of the room
provides a necessary light for
a display of paintings placed in
the piers between window apertures
and on the other walls. Put on
display in this room are canvases
by Italian, Flemish and Dutch
artists of the seventeenth and
eighteenth centuries. The Picture
Gallery of the Pavlovsk Palace,
which reflects the tastes of Paul I
and Maria Fiodorovna, is a traditional formal interior typical of
eighteenth-century royal and grand-
ducal residences.

*The Picture Gallery*

*The Italian Hall*

The Boudoir of Maria Fiodorovna is remarkable in the suite of private Imperial apartments of the Pavlovsk Palace for its elegance and luxurious decor. Small in size, the interior resembles a porcelain casket in which eighteenth-century toilet items are preserved. The walls of the Boudoir are rhythmically covered with elaborate arabesques simulating Raphael's painted designs in the loggias of the Vatican Palace. The space of the walls between the pilasters is covered with ancient Roman reliefs and painted landscapes. Two large marble bas-reliefs represent Alexander the Great and his mother Olympia. This is an allusion, in an allegorical form, to the future Emperor Alexander I and his mother Maria Fiodorovna. Of spe-cial mention is a magnificent marble fireplace with columns of Roman work that is reminiscent of a triumphal arch.

*The Room for the Ladies-in-Waiting*
**Cupid Shooting a Bow**. *1761*
*By Carle van Loo*

*The Boudoir of Maria Fiodorovna*

The Large Throne Room occupying an area of 400 square metres is distinguished for the scale and luxury of its space. Brenna enhanced this effect by introducing into the decor of the interior vast arched apertures and semicircular niches in which he placed stoves with a sumptuous relief decoration. The arched window surrounds adorned with caryatids resemble triumphal arches. The bas-relief depiction of fruit, flowers and musical instruments, indispensable attributes of a royal feast, suggest that the Great Hall was originally intended for festive gatherings. After his ascension Paul I ordered that the Great Hall be used as the Throne Room. Then a special place decorated with velvet drapery trimmed with gold braids was arranged against the closed window to accommodate the Imperial throne.

Worthy of interest is the painting of the ceiling made after a sketch by Pietro Gonzago. However, the concept of the great monumental painter was not realized. It was only in 1971, during restoration, that the ceiling of the Throne Room was adorned with the author's original design. The painting not only produced an illusion of a larger interior, but also returned a triumphal character to it complementing the room's architectonics with painted representations of a classical colonnade, hanging standards of the Guards and the St Andrew flag of the Russian Navy.

Exhibited in the Large Throne Room is a unique Guryev Service produced in 1817 at the St Petersburg Imperial Porcelain Factory specially for the Pavlovsk Palace. The porcelain groups for table decoration were modelled by Stepan Pimenov. The crystal items of the service produced in England are very rare examples of artistic glasswork dating from the late eighteenth century.

*The Great Throne Hall*
*(The State Dining Room)*

*The Great Throne Room. Girandole*
*Late 18th century. The Imperial Glass Works,*
*St Petersburg*

The Grecian Hall is one of those works of architecture the harmony of which evokes lofty artistic associations. It might be called a hymn to the art of Ancient Greece. The inclusion into the decor of the interior of Corinthian columns, stuccowork and sculpture illustrates the designer's deep penetration into the essence of ancient artistic traditions. The hall designed by Brenna was also enriched with architectural elements added later into the decor of the interior by Voronikhin. The sixteen marine-coloured columns of artificial marble, the rich moulded decor of the ceiling, the low vault and the marble bowl lamps, all adds to the slender and festive look of the hall. The two fireplaces of white marble which had been manufac-tured for the Mikhailovsky Palace were brought to Pavlovsk in 1803 by Voronikhin who retained the stylistic integrity of the Grecian Hall.

*The Third Anteroom. Clock*
*Second half of the 18th century*
*Workshop of Pierre Caron*

*The Grecian Hall*

*Clock:* **Helen and Paris**
*Late 18th century*
*Workshop of L. J. Laguesse,*
*Liège, France*

*The he State Bedroom of the Empress Maria Fiodorovna designed by Vincenzo Brenna is notable for the extreme luxury of its decoration. The walls of the room are lined with silk panels painted in bright colours. Their motifs are symbols of idyllic pastoral life at one with nature. The same subject matter dominates the ceiling painting which imitates a garden trellis interwoven with flowers. The most prominent feature of the State Bedroom is the sumptuous bed lavishly decorated with gilded ornamental carving and sculptures — allegories of happiness and prosperity of the royal family. The furniture set of a canopied bed, coach and armchairs is a master-work produced by Henri Jacob, one of the most outstanding French cabinet-makers.

The Little Lantern Study, a truly inspired work by Voronikhin, is perceived as an antithesis to the pomposity of the Bedroom. A blend of painting, sculpture, colour and light creates an impression that the Little Lantern is not only a palatial interior but a place of solitary contemplation and a "home of the Muses".

*The State Bedroom*

*The Little Lantern Study*

$\mathcal{T}$he Pavlovsk Park is a kind of a philosophical poem about the essence of spiritual life, its secrets, joys and serene melancholy. The chapters of this poem are picturesque views of the park usually animated by a pavilion, a decorative structure or a sculpture. The Apollo Colonnade is interesting not only in terms of artistic perfection bringing forth associations with Classical Antiquity, but also for its architectural biography. In 1783 Cameron erected an open double-ring Doric colonnade at the entrance to the park and set up a statue of *Apollo Belvedere*, a copy from Leochares' original, in the centre of it. The colonnade became the emblem of Pavlovsk as an abode of poetry and art. In 1800 the Colonnade was shifted to the high bank of the Slavianka and installed along the slope of the landscaped Cascade. In 1817, during a thunderstorm, part of the Colonnade collapsed which, however, only emphasized its romantic look. The Pavilion of the Three Graces put up by Cameron in 1800–01 is also an interpretation of an ancient architectural motif. The pavilion was erected at the axis of the main avenue of Her Majesty's Own Garden laid out in the style of French regular parks. It was adorned with a marble group by the eighteenth-century Italian sculptor Paolo Triscorni. The sculptural group revealing Triscorni's consummate mastery of marble treatment is an expressive version of an ancient original with the image of the three deities personifying female beauty.

Sculpture is an almost indispensable part of the park structures. Marble and cast-iron lions embellish the Large Stone (Italian) Staircase designed by Brenna. The marble statues look particularly attractive against the greenery of the park. Especially notable among them is *Erminia* by Rinaldo Rinaldi created in the middle of the nine-teenth century.

*The Apollo Colonnade*

*Sculpture:* ***Erminia****. Mid-19th century Sculptor Rinaldo Rinaldi*

*The Pavilion of the Three Graces*

*The Large Stone (Italian) Staircase*

ensemble of this kind is the Twelve Walks area, with the bronze representations of the Muses, patrons of the arts and sciences (copies from ancient originals) surrounding the statue of Apollo. A typical example is *Clio*, the Muse of History, cast by Edmonde Gastecloux at the St Petersburg Academy of Arts, where all of them were produced.

*The Temple of Friendship. 1780–82*

*The Peel Tower. 1795–97*

*The Old Sylvia. The Twelve Walks area*
*Clio, the Muse of History. 1794. Russia*
*Cast by Edmonde Gastecloux. Copy from*
*an ancient original of the 3rd century B.C.*

*T*he Temple of Friendship is the earliest pavilion structure built by Cameron in Pavlovsk. This perfect work is outstanding not only for the complex of the Pavlovsk Park, but is a masterpiece of eighteenth-century Russian Classicism as a whole. Drawing on the forms of ancient architecture, Cameron attained a striking harmony and succeeded in endowing the pavilion with a special spiritual atmosphere. In this sense Cameron could be compared with Gavriil Derzhavin who, carrying out the "most august commission", infused his verses with true inspiration.

The pavilion is dedicated by Paul and his wife Maria Fiodorovna to Empress Catherine the Great. The inscription over the doors,

"With love, reverence and gratitude devoted", alludes to this fact, as do the allegorical relief medallions Glory, Friendship, Gratitude, Justice and the traditional symbols of friendly feelings — dolphins, wreathes and vines.

The emphasized rustic simplicity of the Pavlovsk Park was enhanced by decorative pavilions. The romantic image of a peeling mill with a dilapidating tower (hence its name, the Peel Tower), built to a design by Brenna and decorated with painting by Gonzago, was a sort of theatrical mask of the palatial pavilion.

Its upper floor was used as a hotel for repose and enjoyment of the scenery. The sculptural decoration of the Pavlovsk Park is thematically united. The most well-known

The Pavlovsk Park had a memorial character from the first years of its existence. In one of its quiet corners, at the wish of Paul I and Maria Fiodorovna, the Monument to the Parents of the Empress shaped as a semi-rotunda pavilion was erected. While the Monument to the Parents reflects an elegiac mood, another commemorative structure, the Mausoleum, conveys the depth of Maria Fiodorovna's suffering after the assassination of her husband, Emperor Paul I.

The inscription on the pediment reads: *To My Spouse and Benefactor*. The architect Jean-François Thomas de Thomon and the sculptor Ivan Martos, contemporaries of the palatial coup, created an image of grief at the loss — not so much of the Emperor as of the beloved man, father and the head of the family, the first owner of the Pavlovsk palace-and-park complex. These feelings of solitude and mournful sorrow are expressed in the austere architecture of the ancient temple decorated with four monolithic columns, in the emphasized monumental volume of the cella, in the monotonous rustication of the walls and especially in the frieze. The allegorical masks of tragedy with closed eyes and frozen tears symbolize eternal laments about the victim of assassination and a mute reproach to those who broke human laws.

The banks of the Slavianka River are effectively emphasized by bridges. The Visconti Bridge is especially prominent for its expressive forms, its monumental vases and the beauty of its arched span.

*The Pavilion "To My Spouse and Benefactor"*

*The Visconti Bridge*

*The Palace. View from the Slavianka River*

# Oranienbaum

The name of Oranienbaum (German for "orange-tree"), the estate of Alexander Menshikov, Peter the Great's companion-in-arms, stresses a private rather than formal character of the summer residence of the influential courtier. The earliest mention of the site goes back to the beginning of the eighteenth century when a Finnish-Swedish farmstead on the south shore of the Gulf of Finland near the estuary of the Karost River became Menshikov's property. In 1707 a construction of his country residence began on this site. Three years later the architect Giovanni Fontana began to erect a stone palace and to lay out a regular garden. He was replaced by Johann-Gottfried Schädel who supervised all the prince's architectural projects. From January 1725 to September 1727 the Oranienbaum residence glistened almost with a royal brilliance which corresponded to the position of Russia's "half-ruling sovereign". In 1743 Oranienbaum became the summer residence of Grand Duke Piotr Fiodorovich (the future Emperor Peter III) and his wife Yekaterina Alexeyevna (the future Empress Catherine the Great). Almost for ten years the construction at Oranienbaum was supervised by Rastrelli. In 1756 the owners entrusted Antonio Rinaldi with the architectural development of the residence. To satisfy the unusual tastes of Grand Duke Piotr Fiodorovich, he created the Peterstadt Fortress. In 1762–74 the architect united the Oranienbaum structures into a single ensemble for Catherine the Great. It included the Chinese Palace, the Coasting Hill with a pavilion and a park with numerous bridges and a variety of decorative structures. Happily not occupied during the War of 1941–45, Oranienbaum, unlike the other suburban residences of St Petersburg, has retained its original artistic appearance.

The Chinese Palace created by Rinaldi in 1762–68 is distinguished for the perfect finish and refined luxury of its interior decor. The symmetrical volumes of the palace contain the state rooms and halls fanciful in composition and absolutely individual in their artistic decoration (the Great Hall, the Hall of the Muses and the Great Chinese Study), as well as the drawing

← 
*The Chinese Palace. View from the pond*

*The Great Chinese Study*

*The Buglework Room*

rooms and living apartments of Catherine the Great and her son Paul. The three state rooms of the palace are especially remarkable because the subjects of their ceiling paintings and the motifs of their parquet designs and fabric patterns were borrowed from Chinese art (hence the present-day name of the palace). Especially resplendent is the Great Chinese Study. Its walls are faced with wooden inlaid panels which include ivory plaques representing *chinoiserie* motifs. A veritable treasure of decorative art is the Buglework Room. Its walls are adorned with twelve panels embroi-

dered in silk against a beadwork background. The panels feature fantastical landscapes of tropical woods inhabited by birds and decorated with small bridges and pavilions.

The interiors of the palace appear as an entity thanks to its inlaid floors, painted ceilings and pictures produced by such well-known Italian artists as Stefano Torelli, Francesco Zugno, Francesco Zuccarelli, Gasparo Dizziani, Giacomo Cignarolli, Giuseppe and Serafino Barozzi, Jacopo Guarano, Giovanni-Battista Pittoni and Domenico Maggiotto.

*C*oasting hills, used to slide down in sledges in winter and in special cars in summer, were a popular entertainment in the eighteenth century. Nowadays only the pavilion created by Rinaldi survives from the Oranienbaum Coasting Hill. The largest interior of the pavilion is a round hall adorned with decorative moulding and painting. The unique floor is made of artificial marble with a fanciful painted ornament. The Porcelain Study is remarkable for its moulded decor which include the figurines of monkeys and birds supporting shelves with Meissen porcelain pieces.

*The Coasting Hill Pavilion*

*The Round Hall of the Coasting Hill Pavilion*

*The Porcelain Study. Porcelain composition:*
**The Triumph of Venus. 1772–74**

The remains of Peterstadt, or Peter's city, differ from other landmarks of the Oranienbaum complex by the unusual purpose for which it was constructed. It was a small fortress built in keeping with the latest achievements of eighteenth-century fortification. The toy fortress was provided with everything necessary for real military manoeuvres and for war games which were the favourite entertainment of its owner, at that time the heir to the throne, Grand Duke Piotr Fiodorovich. Nowadays only the Honourary Gate and the Palace of Peter III have survived from the structures designed by Rinaldi. Although the toy fortress was believed to have a defensive significance and was recorded in the War Ministry, the palace of the Commander-in-Chief of Peterstadt was marked by a sumptuous, distinctly state design of its interiors.

The walls of the Large Study or Picture Gallery, the most representative interior in the palace, were covered from top to bottom with sixty-three canvases by Western European artists of the seventeenth and eighteenth centuries, while the lower portions of the walls were decorated with lacquer panels showing painted scenes on fashionable Chinese subjects (imitated by the master craftsman Fiodor Vlasov). Peter III spent his last days as the Emperor, before he was dethroned by his mutinous wife, in this palace. Surrounded by the Holstein regiments, he was waiting for the fateful news from St Petersburg without taking any resolute measures to save his position.

*The Palace of Peter III*

*The Palace of Peter III*
*The Large Study (the Picture Hall)*

*The Honourary Gate leading to Peterstadt*

# Gatchina

Gatchina, the name of both the town and the palace-and-park ensemble, dates back to distant times. It probably derives from the Russian expression *gat' chinit'*, that is "to repair a road with poles" or from the German *hat schöne*, "to be beautiful". In the late fifteenth century a Russian village already existed here, which in 1712, after the eventual annexation of the Izhora lands to Russia, the area was presented by Peter the Great to his sister, Tsarevna Natalia Alexeyevna. During the subsequent years Gatchina had different owners. In 1765 Catherine the Great bought Gatchina for the state and presented it to her favourite Count Grigory Orlov, as a reward for his major role in the palatial coup of 1762. Orlov possessed Gatchina from 1766 to 1783. During this period

Antonio Rinaldi put up a palace for him, laid out a park and decorated it with obelisks and monuments in honour of the Orlovs' deeds. In 1783 Catherine the Great presented Gatchina to her son, Grand Duke Pavel Petrovich and his consort. For thirty years Gatchina was the grand-ducal estate and in 1796–1801 it became the Imperial residence. During these years Vincenzo Brenna redecorated the palace and put up a number of new structures, such as the Eagle and Venus Pavilions, the portal of the Birch House and the Connetable Obelisk. In the late eighteenth and early nineteenth centuries active in Gatchina were Vasily Bazhenov, Nikolai Lvov and Andreyan Zakharov, who completed this grand ensemble of the eighteenth and nineteenth centuries.

The Gatchina Palace originally was a hunting lodge of Grigory Orlov, a favourite of Catherine the Great. Later it became a residence of the Russian Emperors Paul I, Nicholas I, Alexander II and Alexander III. It is remarkable not only as a work of art, but also as a witness to many most important historical events, political and intimate secrets of the royal family. The palace-castle was erected on the ridge of a hill. Its north front is oriented towards the tract of greenery which skirts the mirror-like lakes and stretches to the foot of the slope. The south front is opened up to the parade ground intended for the guard mounting and exemplary military exercises. Alongside the outer border of the parade ground runs a low bastion war or parapet pierced with embrasures for cannons. The ditch around the palace emphasizes its resemblance to a castle. The volume of the palace is marked by a clear-cut silhouette and is accentuated by the pentagonal five-tiered Guard and Signal Towers. Faced with plaques and blocks of greyish-silvery and golden Pudost stone, the palace seems to be enveloped in a light haze enhancing a romantic aura of the entire edifice.

Three basic periods are clearly traced in the architectural history of the Gatchina Palace: 1765–81 — the construction and decoration of the castle for Orlov to Rinaldi's designs; the 1790s — minor alterations to Brenna's drawings in the volumes of the lateral sections and redesigning of the state interiors for Paul I and his wife; 1845–56 — the period when the architect Roman Kuzmin added the new square wings where the apartments of Nicholas I and members of his family and the premises of the court services were located.

*←*

*The Gatchina Palace and the Parade Ground*

*The White Dining Room*

*The Anteroom*

The state apparatus of the Gatchina Palace were located in the central block on the first floor. They were badly damaged during the Second World War. Some of them have been reconstructed and are open for visitors. The Marble (Dining) Hall created by Brenna attracts by its sense of space, this effect being enhanced by the white artificial marble used in the decor of the walls and the sixteen fluted marble columns.

The Anteroom (Reception Room) leads to the State Suite which is notable for a restrained plastic decor. The decoration of the Anteroom has retained some elements of the original design made by Antonio Rinaldi for Count Orlov — the painted ceiling, the moulded ornaments and the inlaid parquet floor with its pattern resembling an openwork flower.

The Throne Room of Paul I was arranged in the former study of Count Orlov. Brenna gave this small interior a grand appearance adorning it with stately details. First of all, the throne was installed on a special pediment in the pier between the windows. The walls were lined with picturesque eighteenth-century tapestries. The ceiling of the Throne Room was embellished with bands and geometric insets of classical ornamentation, their relief decoration being stressed by three-dimensional gilding. Redesigning the study into the Throne Room, Brenna paid particular attention to the ancient Roman military symbols — he added to the decor the single-headed eagle with which

*The Throne Room of Paul I*

*The Throne Room
of Empress Maria Fiodorovna*

*The Crimson Drawing Room*

*The Throne of Emperor Alexander III*

the standards of the Roman legions were crowned. Brenna deliberately made the doors and overdoor decorations sumptuous and imposing. Having retained Rinaldi's parquet floor, the architect perfectly solved the complex compositional problem.

In keeping with the etiquette of the royal court, Empress Maria Fiodorovna had her own Throne Room in the suite of her private apartments. Its walls were lined with crimson cloth and decorated with paintings selected so as to suit the principle of symmetry. Similarly to the other state rooms, Brenna adorned the doors, window surrounds and overdoor decorative panels of Maria Fiodorovna's Throne Room with an exquisite luxury. The major decorative feature of this Throne Room is the marble fireplace adorned with relief insets featuring ancient images. One of the most sumptuous interiors in the Gatchina Palace is the Crimson Drawing Room. Brenna embellished its walls with tapestries executed at the French Royal Manufacture in 1776–1780s. The tapestries were

diplomatic presents to Grand Duke Pavel Petrovich and his consort during their visit to Paris in 1782. The tapestries show scenes illustrating episodes from the novel *Don Quixote* by Cervantes (*Ladies Attending the Knight*). The colour range and ornamental patterns of the tapestries were matched by the gilded moulding of the ceiling and especially by the decor of the door panels and painted overdoor decorations.

The last crowned owner of Gatchina was Emperor Alexander III. "The Gatchina recluse" — this is how the father of the last Russian monarch was nicknamed for his love to the romantic Gatchina scenery. Now visitors to the palace can see the gilded throne of Alexander III which reminds them about the dramatic history of the Gatchina Palace. Gatchina had not lost the significance of the main Imperial summer residence until the end of the nineteenth century.

*The White Hall*

*The State Bedroom*
*Ceiling Painting: **The Wedding of Psyche***
*By Gabriel François Doyen*
*Late 18th century*

*T*he White Hall situated in the central part of the palace charms visitors by its sense of space. Its five huge semicircular French windows lead to the balcony which affords a splendid view of the Parade Ground that served as the venue for a picturesque ceremony of guard mounting. The hall owes its name to the colour scheme of its walls. Brenna put the main plastic emphasis in his design of the hall on thirty-two Corinthian pilasters. The ceiling of the White Hall is accentuated by the painted scene produced by Gabriel-François Doyen. It matches the beautiful inlaid parquet floor executed to drawings by Rinaldi and left intact by Brenna during his redecoration of the White Hall in the late eighteenth century. Worthy of especial interest is the collection of ancient sculpture and the bas-reliefs by well-known sculptors of the seventeenth and the first half of the eighteenth centuries.

The White Hall served as a fine setting for palatial balls, festivals and the "state entries of the Imperial family", during which sumptuous garments of court ladies, gentlemen and guards officers glistened against the exquisite architecture.

The Gatchina Park has been laid out around several lakes which occupy a third part of its area. It was created in 1766–83 after Rinaldi's drawings and completed in 1783–1800 under the supervision of Brenna. The composition of the palatial park consists of a number of gardens, both regular and landscaped ones, each of which has an artistic solution of its own. A large portion of the park is taken by the English-style garden laid out around the White and Silver Lakes. The combination of the smooth water surface, the vivid play of light and the reflections of the beautiful bank landscapes animated by the silhouettes of the palace, pavilions and smaller structures; all adds a musical quality to the atmosphere reigning the park, which has been defined as a "symphony of the North". All kinds of bridges, gates and pavilions are set into the scenery of the park, but worthy of particular note are some of them which remind of the great accomplishments of the Orlov brothers, children of an officer of Peter's army, who became famous during the reign of Catherine the Great. The Eagle (or Temple) Pavilion put up in 1792 on the bank of the so-called Long Island is one of these structures. It was surmounted with the figure of a crowned eagle. The royal bird was supposed to symbolize the Orlov family (their surname derives from the Russian word for "eagle"), an allegory of their high predestination. The Chesme Obelisk erected after drawings by Rinaldi is a memorial in honour of the victory of the Russian fleet under the command of Count Alexey Orlov-Chesmensky.

*The Eagle (Temple) Pavilion*

*The Prior's Palace. 1799. Architect Nikolai Lvov. View from the White Lake*

*The Chesme Obelisk*

Text by Grigory Yar
Translated from the Russian by Valery Fateyev
Designed by Yevgeny Gavrilov
Art editor Nikolai Kutovoi
Cover design by Denis Lazarev
Editor-in-Chief Sergei Vesnin
Edited by Maria Lyzhenkova
Computer layout by Yelena Morozova
Colour correction by Liubov Kornilova
Photographs by Valentin Baranovsky, Valery Barnev, Leonid Bogdanov, Vladimir Davydov, Pavel Demidov,
Vladimir Denisov, Konstantin Doka, Natalia Doka, Vladimir Dorokhov, Alexander Gronsky,
Artur Kirakozov, Boris Manushin, Vladimir Melnikov, Yury Molodkovets, Victor Savik, Georgy Shablovsky,
Vladimir Shlakan, Yevgeny Siniaver, Oleg Trubsky, Vladimir Vdovin, Vasily Vorontsov, Vadim Yegorovsky
Managing Editor Maria Lyzhenkova

ISBN 5-900530-97-3

Printed and bound by the Ivan Fiodorov Printing Company, St Petersburg (No 1401)